Lasso the Wind

AURÉLIA'S VERSES and OTHER POEMS

text by GEORGE ELLIOTT CLARKE

illustrations by SUSAN TOOKE

NIMBUS
PUBLISHING
nimbus.ca

"Time was," the golden head
Irrevocably said;
But time which none can bind,
While flowing fast away, leaves love behind.
—Robert Louis Stevenson

Hold in high poetic duty,
Truest Truth the fairest Beauty.
—Elizabeth Barrett Browning

❧

Nimbus Publishing Limited
3731 Mackintosh St, Halifax, NS B3K 5A5
(902) 455-4286 nimbus.ca

Printed and bound in China

Cover and interior design: Heather Bryan
Author photo: Camelia Linta
Illustrator photo: Richard Rudnicki
Reference photos of Aurélia: Julie Morin

Library and Archives Canada Cataloguing in Publication

Clarke, George Elliott, 1960-, author
Lasso the wind : Aurélia's verses and other poems / George Elliott Clarke ; illustrations by Susan Tooke.

Illustrated poetry collection.
Reading grade level: For middle-grade readers.
Issued in print and electronic formats.
ISBN 978-1-77108-050-7 (bound).
ISBN 978-1-77108-051-4 (pdf)

1. Children's poetry, Canadian (English). I. Tooke, Susan, illustrator II. Title.

PS8555.L3748L38 2013   jC811'.54
C2013-903452-8
C2013-903453-6

Nimbus Publishing acknowledges the financial support for its publishing activities from the Government of Canada through the Canada Book Fund (CBF) and the Canada Council for the Arts, and from the Province of Nova Scotia through the Department of Communities, Culture and Heritage.

 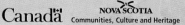 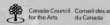

For Aurélia

This book was born in sea-bright Halifax
When Susan Tooke, artist, dispatched a fax
Requesting lyrics, *inter alia*:
At once I thought of you, Aurélia.
You are quite chasteningly critical
And precociously analytical,
And yet I pray, my daughter, that you'll see
How much your opinions matter to me.

I lounged in trattoria or café,
To craft these poems, part-deft, part-daffy,
To perhaps see you and a stranger smile,
To muse on this amusement for a while.
Soon you will compose some books all your own—
And if praise I hear, yours is the renown.

       —George Elliott Clarke

For my grandchildren, Lexie, Jevin, and Anthony,
  with love.   —Susan Tooke

Can you burn down the sun?
Can you darken the moon?
Can you drown a mountain?
Can you bid stars to swoon?

Can you lasso the wind?
Can you whip it a-gale?
Can you make oceans bend
To cradle each lost whale?

When you picnic with a dragon,
Bring oranges, meat, and ginger ale:
Each sips pop straight from a flagon,
And must munch fruit and snack on snail.

Soup from dirty underwear—
Dishes of worms and flies—
And mud mixed well with vinegar:
I serve to all my enemies.

A snake passes;
The field rumbles.

A cloud masses;
Down rain tumbles.

New leaves! New leaves!
Spring is busy
Greening earth's eaves.
Brooks go dizzy;
Robins delight.
Everything's green
That once was white.
Butterflies preen;
Gilt lilies flute.
All blossoms sing,
Now rain takes root.
Each queen and king
Slow promenades,
In skirts and pants
Cross dales and glades,
Where sunbeams dance
On wings and webs,
And light green sleeves,
While chill air ebbs
To leaves, new leaves!

Glory is grass
Basking in sun:
Smile at troubles,
And trouble's done.

Once it is plucked,
The rose must fade.
But thorns aren't tricked—
And prick the glad.

When governors order brand-new jails,
Voters should expect to cram those cells:
Imprison their children and their spouses
And empty out their cribs, beds, and houses.

It is so appalling to be poor,
One begs and begs, door to peep-holed door.
And when dry crust of bread is given,
One must kneel and shout thanks to Heaven.

The sky
Is no bigger than what my eye
Can see,
And the sun is smaller than me.

When a cloud covers the sun,
It covers everyone.

Espied through rain—or through stained-glass,
A street shimmers just like Venice.

Rain thrashes, trembles, through branches—
Gusty, lusty avalanches—
Pure fluid—April's pearls—downfall,
Demolishing snow, ice, and all.

April Song

Chirrup, chirrup, chirrup!
Chirp! Chirp! Chirp!
Sing *Spring,* sap and syrup;
Let babes burp.

Lambs gambol and ramble.
Cocks crow dawn.
Mares at crossroads amble,
Then prance on.

Crocus crack through snow crust,
Crackling tints;
Dazzle displaces dust:
Jazz brilliance!

Chirrup, chirrup, chirrup!
Chirp! Chirp! Chirp!
Sing *Spring,* sap and syrup;
Let babes burp.

A black-and-amber butterfly
Ushers April to my door:
Light increases the fleecy sky,
And floods from roof to floor.

When woods are green
And blossoms white,
I imagine
Sugary light.

And babes all pipe
Their raucous glee—
The holy type
That's Liberty.

Sport is best when no score is kept,
And those who lose are those who slept,
When the sun illuminated
Playgrounds where no refs awaited.

True children always wish to play—
Even when night replaces day—
Their laughter keeps the moon awake
Until cock crow and dawn must break.

The ocean's a lot of brittle foam
That makes to stay, but makes no home.
It looks like marble under light,
Or suave velvet set soaking wet.
I like the salt it leaves once dry—
As spice from Greece or Italy—
Or how it coddles when I swim,
And bounces every buoyant limb.
I think it's better than the sky
Because it's closer—motherly—
And keeps us clean as spotless priests
And sinks dead-weight philosophies.

Waves whittle the horizon down
Until the sun descends to drown.

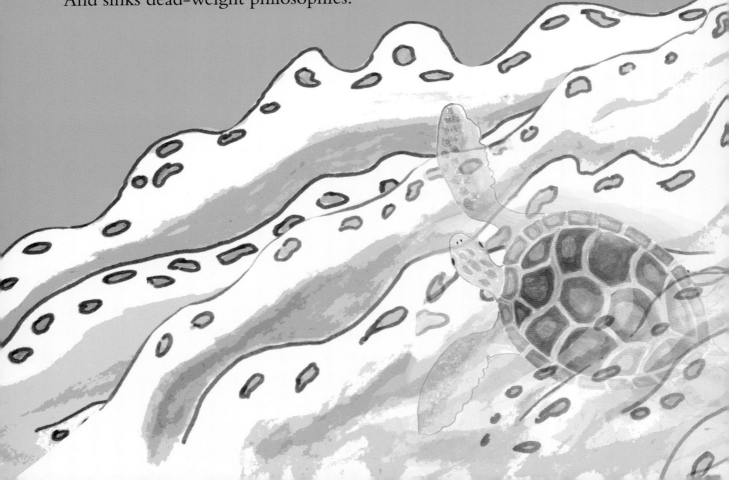

At the oasis of the elephants,
Giraffes canter and hippos prance.

A zebra is prison bars gone free—
Zoology sketches Liberty.

The dreadful lion need not roar:
It munches meat that bleats no more.
Its jaws are silent as it chews,
Its belly's purring sweetest joys.

Once we're asleep, free we voyage
Among memory and image,
And fancy every different thing
Of Imagination's making,
And anchor among shadows grand,
And make of light itself our land,
Where birdsong serves as our scripture
And dew debuts dawning rapture.

Pirates with parrots voyage all around,
Eyeballing islands where gold can be found,
Without looking—or digging—very hard;
But I measure treasure in my backyard.

My kingdom can be a plot of grass
No wider than my resting arse.
From here I can eye the universe,
Using a magnifying glass.

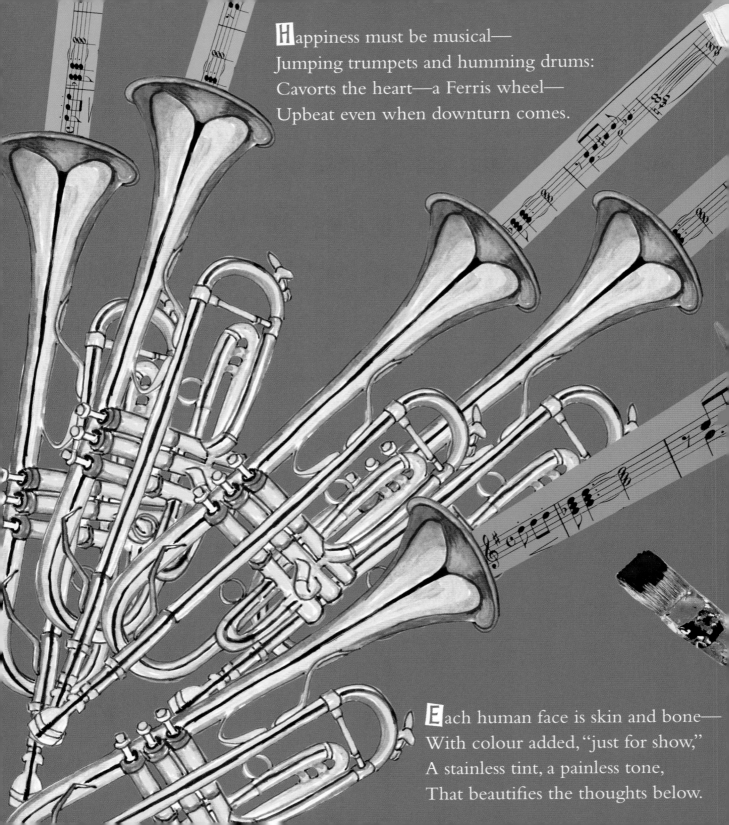

Happiness must be musical—
Jumping trumpets and humming drums:
Cavorts the heart—a Ferris wheel—
Upbeat even when downturn comes.

Each human face is skin and bone—
With colour added, "just for show,"
A stainless tint, a painless tone,
That beautifies the thoughts below.

Ebony and ivory, the piano
Whips up melody from black ink
and snow.

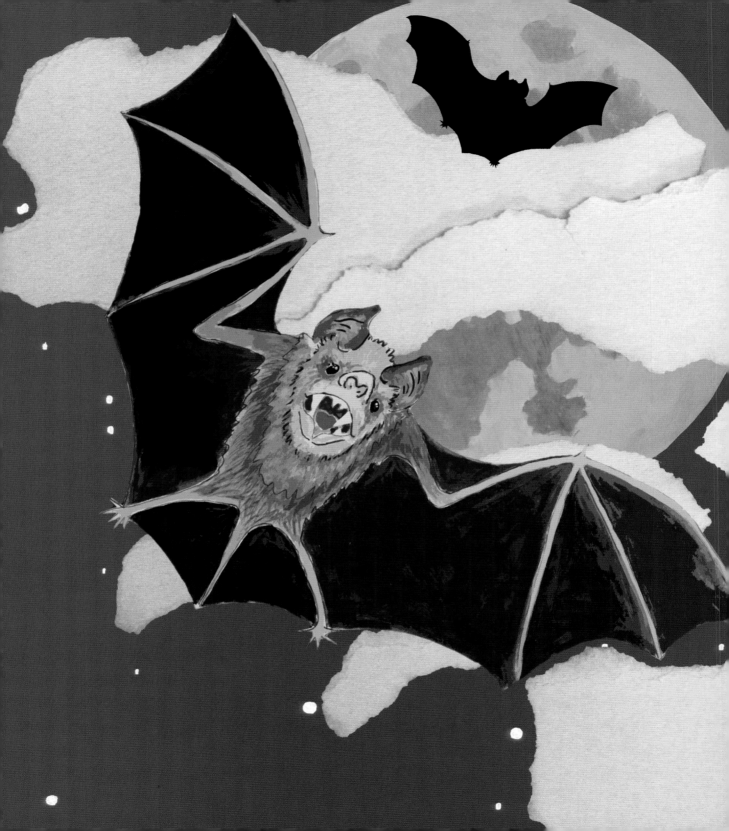

Dracula is no different than Cupid:
One is batty; the other is stupid.
One bares fangs, but the other bears arrows.
Both wing and swoop to snare you in sorrows.

That a bee's fit to fly,
Defies all logic
Aerodynamically,
But Nature's magic.

A bumblebee zigzags through air
Because honey's everywhere.

A fly is crude in etiquette—
His fine table is his toilet.
For manners, he prefers to wash
His filthy lips in dirt and slosh.

What's best about winter is my bed—
Flannel-sheeted and woollen-blanketed.
Once tucked in tight, I look out the window
Upon heavy heaving or heaping snow.
I almost shiver when seeing these things,
But comfy I am while the hoot-owl wings.

That sugary whiteness of the moon:
Snow scooped up by a silver spoon.

Blow trumpet! Beat a drum!
Enter Byzantium!
Princesses dance and sway—
Like palm trees—all the day.
Roses—so red they scald—
Nod near rivers emerald.
Pirates—each rat-eye a-gleam—
Drown deep in chocolate ice cream.
Brooding, copper, and big—
The figment of a fig—
The sun surrenders soon
That vivid pearl, the moon,
So bright fires freeze to ice
And diamonds turn to rice
Pudding, a milky way—
Or sugar-star display.
All saints, know your duty:
Sorrow clouds up Beauty.
Blast trumpet! Bang a drum!
Enter Byzantium!

In sleep, I have my freedom still.
Awake, I pace a prison cell.
But my own jail is nothing real,
Just my ideals impractical.

When proud palms do promenade,
The sun, too, goes on parade.

The sunflower beams its summer light,
Denying ever winter night.
But in its shade, now drooping black,
Sly Jack Frost stoops, poised to attack.

School is a cell of books and teacher-guards.
Emancipation? Recess and schoolyards.

Jealousy is a sulking fiend,
Skulking in disguise of friend.
The face is smiles, the praise is sound:
No nicer enemy is found.

Trouble bubbles when problems stew,
Until Catastrophe's the brew.

Toss out the mess and start again
Before Calamities happen.

A headline
Is a deadline
That's come and gone.
News: Damage done.

The tears of a chameleon
Mirror drops of watermelon.

No matter how pretty he is,
A peacock still eats crumbs.
He chews dirt while looking gorgeous,
But pebbles just aren't plums.

The great gift of eyesight
Is to spy stars at night—
In dozens—or thousands—
While our hearts make amends
For wrongs we wrought today
When, blind, we looked away
From light and stumbled through
Mazes, crooked, narrow.

The stars are martial beams—
A battlefield's watch—
Impervious to our dreams—
And every prayer we botch.

Each one eyes us coldly—
Like vultures winging high,
Then swooping down boldly,
To strip us thoroughly.

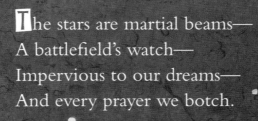

It's today
That I can see
Daisies play
At being me.

Beaming gold,
They bend and sway—
Limber, bold,
Anarchic, gay.

Holding out
Their leaves like hands,
They don't shout
Or make demands.

They're quiet,
Quite, but not shy:
Their riot
Is their beauty.

If I seem
A weed to some
Eyes, I dream—
And flower I am.

AURÉLIA'S VERSES

Le Jour de la Bastille

At 8:10 p.m., you appeared—
all 7 pounds, 11 ounces,
or 3,490 grams,
and you did not cry.

Pure gold was the July 14th sun
at that hour, that height.

You had lots of hair atop a high forehead,
You did not cry.

You smiled instead,
and cast a scrutinizing glance,
behaving as critically
as an artist.

Your eyes turned toward the sun, golden,
burning.

(Up until you appeared,
the sky was uncertainly sunny,
just blue–white–grey,
revolutionary.

Then you were coming,
with your fierce heart drumming!)

Year One

You are no simple spirit,
Though robed in flesh and light:
An emissary of Beauty,
Revolutionary as Gospel.

One year old, how can you know
The beginning that you are?
Alert, you speak to the sky,
And no one causes you tears.

Year Two

You are a beautiful poem
In a new language, a *sound* song.
My heart has been two years your home,
And here you always will belong.

I compose words like a poet;
But I'm your "Pa'," a better part,
And more important. I know it,
But Love requires no scholar's art.

Year Three

Svelte, indignant Creole—
Black Mi'kmaq, Québécoise—
True, mid-life miracle,
You are Time's pure applause.

Year Four

Dear darling daughter—
Joint Nova Scotia-and-Québec,
"Negro" is your laughter,
Part Mi'kmaq and part–italic.

I pray you will mature—
Mirthful, feisty, and proud as fire—
Blend Art into Nature,
With undaunted, expert aspire.

Year Five

You are five—and laughing so much—
Plus talking back to everyone!

But you are right to be so blithe:
How else can you know Adventure?

Year Seven

Bicycle again through the mud,
Then skip, somehow unscathed, through thorns.
White blossoms into apples bud,
And girl musicians all blast horns.

You crackle books—see lightning crack—
As explosive as a cannon.
Each page spells magic, white and black—
Words in starry constellation.

Dance like iambs and anapests—
Sprightly; ignore Gravity's laws.
Be like rain, plain, but boisterous.
Your smile wins cascades of applause.

Year Nine

Aurélia, Star, reflect the light
Of Reason, Wisdom, and of Wit—
Look to stars and sunflowers at
   night,
And, for sunlight, see Holy Writ.

Writ in Papeete (Tahiti); Istanbul (Turkey); Rodos (Greece); Bucharest (Rumania); Cairo (Egypt); Southampton (Bermuda); Cable Beach (The Bahamas); Halifax (Nova Scotia); Gatineau (Québec); and Toronto (Ontario), 1998-2012.

I acknowledge the assistance of The Trudeau Foundation, whose Fellowship Prize, which I held 2005-08, enabled me to travel and research and write at leisure. Similar luxury has come to me via the E.J. Pratt Professorship, a great, annual benefit bestowed by Dr. Sonia Labatt and Victoria University, at the University of Toronto.

The first readers of these poems were Riitta Tuohiniemi and Aurélia Morin-Clarke. Their amendments were accepted, and the remaining errors are mine.

I thank Susan Tooke for the idea—and the fine art—for this book as well as Patrick Murphy and Penelope Jackson for urging and editing it along to publication. And I am profoundly grateful to Julie Morin for her exemplary parenthood—and photography, and some of her pictures serve as inspirations here.

—George Elliott Clarke

I would like to thank George Elliott Clarke for his humour, thoughtfulness, and courage in the creation of *Lasso the Wind: Aurélia's Verses and Other Poems*. The verses were both a challenge and a pleasure to illustrate.

As always, I thank my husband and fellow artist Richard Rudnicki, for his love and support.

—Susan Tooke

Note on the Type

The font Bill Clarke Caps, used for the subtitle, was created—hand-drawn and inked—by the author's father, in 1969. Special thanks to Andrew Steeves for providing it to Nimbus for this publication.